Merry Christmas

by Sara Nephew

Table of Contents

Blocks

Quilts

Credits

Unless expressly stated, all the quilts in this book were designed, pieced and quilted by Sara Nephew.
Special thanks to the pattern testers Joan Dawson, Jean Look-Krischano, and Darlene Swenson
Photography....Carl Murray

© Sara Nephew 1997
All rights reserved. No part of this book may be copied or reproduced for commercial use without written permission from Clearview Triangle.

Clearview Triangle
8311 180th St. S.E.
Snohomish, WA 98296-4802
Tel: 360-668-4151
Fax: 360-668-6338
E-mail: clearviewtriangle@compuserve.com

ISBN 0-9621172-5-0

Quick Picture Quilts™

Small Santa

This pattern is given in two different sizes. Be sure the finished square size given at the beginning of the pattern is the same as the finished square size of your quilt. Background fabric needs to be a medium that contrasts well with face, beard, and red fabrics.

Cut for 1 block:

1.	2 red, 1 background and 1 boot	3⅞"	square
2.	2 background	3½" x 6½"	rectangle
3.	2 red and 1 background	3½" x 5"	rectangle
4.	1 background	3½" x 4¼"	rectangle
5.	3 background, 2 boot and 1 white	3½"	square
6.	1 red, 1 background and 1 white	2" x 6½"	rectangle
7.	1 face and 1 beard	2" x 5"	rectangle
8.	6 red, 6 white, 2 belt and 3 background	2" x 3½"	rectangle
9.	1 background	2" x 2¾"	rectangle
10.	5 red, 3 beard, 2 boot, 1 buckle and 1 background	2"	square
11.	4 background	1½"	square
12.	1 red	1¼" x 2"	rectangle

Directions:

1. Cut the 3⅞" squares in half diagonally as shown. Sew the resulting triangles together to make large half-squares in the combinations below.
red-black   make 2
red-background   make 2

2. Place a 3½" background square right sides together with a red-black half-square. Sew diagonally across the seam. Trim outside the stitching to a ¼" seam and press to the background. Make another one of these and trim on the opposite side of the diagonal seam. (left and right hands)

3. Place a red 2" square on one end of the 2" x 3½" background rectangle and sew diagonally as shown. Trim and press to the dark. Place another 2" red square on the other end of the background rectangle and sew the opposite diagonal as shown. Make 2 of these. (elbows)

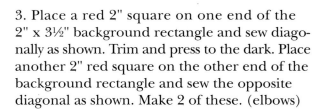

4. Make these pieces:
A. Sew a 2" white square on one corner of a 3½" x 5" red rectangle with a diagonal seam as shown. Trim and press to the dark. Make another with the white square on the opposite corner. (chest)

B. Sew a 2" red square on one corner of the 3½" background square with a diagonal seam as shown.

C. Sew a boot 2" square on one corner of a 3½" x 6½" background rectangle with a diagonal seam as shown. (toe)

D. Sew a boot 2" square on one end of a 2" x 6½" background rectangle with a diagonal seam as shown. (toe)

5. Place a background 2" square on one end of the red 2"x 6½" rectangle and sew a diagonal seam as shown. Outside the stitching, trim fabric to a ¼" seam. Press to the dark. Place the background 2" x 2¾" rectangle on the other end perpendicular to the red rectangle and sew the opposite diagonal seam. Trim and press. (Santa's hat)

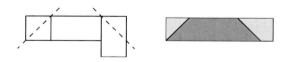

6. Sew the 1½" background squares with diagonal seams on all four corners of the white 3½" square. (ball on Santa's hat)

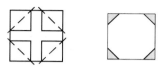

7. Assemble according to the piecing diagram.

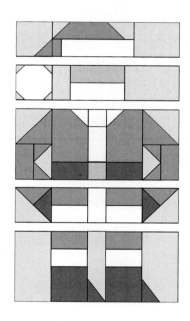

Piecing Diagram

3

Large Santa

This pattern is given in two different sizes. Be sure the finished square size given at the beginning of the pattern is the same as the finished square size of your quilt. Background fabric needs to be a medium that contrasts well with face, beard, and red fabrics.

Cut for 1 block:

1.	2 red, 1 background and 1 boot	4⅞"	square
2.	2 background	4½" x 8½"	rectangle
3.	2 red and 1 background	4½" x 6½"	rectangle
4.	1 background	4½" x 5½"	rectangle
5.	3 background, 2 boot and 1 white	4½"	square
6.	1 red, 1 background and 1 white	2½" x 8½"	rectangle
7.	1 face and 1 white	2½" x 6½"	rectangle
8.	6 red, 6 white, 2 belt and 3 background	2½" x 4½"	rectangle
9.	1 background	2½" x 3½"	rectangle
10.	5 red, 3 beard, 2 boot, 1 buckle, and 1 background	2½"	square
11.	4 background	1¾"	square
12.	1 red	1½" x 2½"	rectangle

Directions:

1. Cut the 4⅞" squares in half diagonally as shown. Sew the resulting triangles together to make large half-squares in the combinations below.
red-black   make 2
red-background   make 2

2. Place a 4½" background square right sides together with a red-black half-square. Sew diagonally across the seam. Trim outside the stitching to a ¼" seam and press to the background. Make another one of these and trim on the opposite side of the diagonal seam. (left and right hands)

3. Place a red 2½" square on one end of the 2½" x 4½" background rectangle and sew diagonally as shown. Trim and press to the dark. Place another 2½" red square on the other end of the background rectangle and sew the opposite diagonal as shown. Make 2 of these. (elbows)

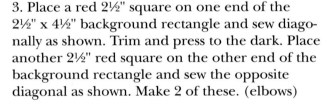

4. Make these pieces:
A. Sew a 2½" white square on one corner of a 4½" x 6½" red rectangle with a diagonal seam as shown. Trim and press to the dark. Make another with the white square on the opposite corner. (chest)

B. Sew a 2½" red square on one corner of the 4½" background square with a diagonal seam as shown.

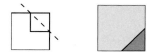

C. Sew a boot 2½" square on one corner of a 4½" x 8½" background rectangle with a diagonal seam as shown. (toe)

D. Sew a boot 2½" square on one end of a 2½" x 8½" background rectangle with a diagonal seam as shown. (toe)

5. Place a background 2½" square on one end of the red 2½" x 8½" rectangle and sew a diagonal seam as shown. Outside the stitching, trim fabric to a ¼" seam. Press to the dark. Place the background 2½" x 3½" rectangle on the other end perpendicular to the red rectangle and sew the opposite diagonal seam. Trim and press. (Santa's hat)

6. Sew the 1¾" background squares with diagonal seams on all four corners of the white 4½" square. (ball on Santa's hat)

7. Assemble according to the piecing diagram.

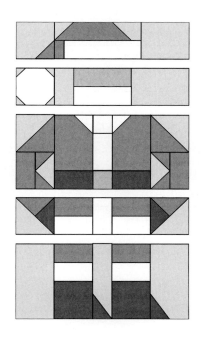

Piecing Diagram

Small Sleigh

1½" finished square
18½" x 21½" block with seam allowance

This pattern is given in two different sizes. Be sure the finished square size given at the beginning of the pattern is the same as the finished square size of your quilt.

Cut for 1 block:

1.	1 background	6½" x 9½"	rectangle
2.	1 sleigh	6½"	square
3.	1 bag	5" x 6½"	rectangle
4.	1 background	5"	square
5.	1 background	3½" x 6½"	rectangle
6.	2 background and 1 bag	3½" x 5"	rectangle
7.	2 background, 1 runner, 1 bag and 1 sleigh	3⅞"	square
8.	4 background, 2 sleigh and 1 ball	3½"	square
9.	1 runner	2" x 18½"	rectangle
10.	1 sleigh	2" x 11"	rectangle
11.	3 background, 2 runner and 2 sleigh	2" x 3½"	rectangle
12.	10 background, 2 candy cane, and 1 runner	2"	square
13.	1 background and 1 candy cane	1¼" x 6"	strip
14.	4 background	1½"	square
15.	2 background	1¼"	square

Directions:

1. Cut the 3⅞" squares in half diagonally as shown. Sew the resulting triangles together to make large half-squares in the combinations below. Make one of each.
sleigh-background
bag-background
runner-background

2. Place a 2" background square right sides together on the runner corner of the runner-background half-square. Sew diagonally, trim outside the stitching to a ¼" seam and press to the background.

3. Place the runner 2" square on one end of a 2" x 3½" background rectangle and sew diagonally as shown.

4. Place a 2" background square on one end of a sleigh 2" x 3½" rectangle and sew a diagonal seam as shown.

5. Place a 2" background square on one end of the 2" x 18½" runner rectangle. Sew a diagonal seam as shown.

6. Sew 2" background squares on the two corners of a long side of the 5" x 6½" bag rectangle with diagonal seams as shown.

7. Sew the 1¼" candy cane and background strips together lengthwise. Cut three 2" sections from this set of strips.

8. Place a candy cane and a background 2" square right sides together and sew a diagonal seam as shown. Outside the stitching, trim fabric to a ¼" seam. Press to the striped fabric. This is a 2" half-square. Then place a 1¼" square on the striped corner of this half square and sew diagonally as shown. Trim and press. Make 2 of these.

9. Sew the 1½" background squares with diagonal seams on all four corners of the ball 3½" square.

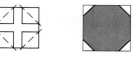

10. Assemble according to the piecing diagram.

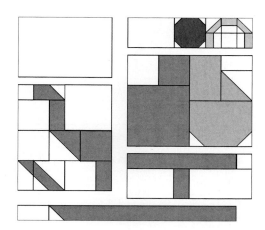

Piecing Diagram

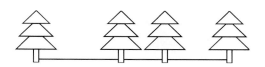

𝓛arge 𝓢leigh

This pattern is given in two different sizes. Be sure the finished square size given at the beginning of the pattern is the same as the finished square size of your quilt.

Cut for 1 block:

1.	1 background	8½" x 12½"	rectangle
2.	1 sleigh	8½"	square
3.	1 bag	6½" x 8½"	rectangle
4.	1 background	6½"	square
5.	1 background	4½" x 8½"	rectangle
6.	2 background and 1 bag	4½" x 6½"	rectangle
7.	2 background, 1 runner, 1 bag and 1 sleigh	4⅞"	square
8.	4 background, 2 sleigh and 1 ball	4½"	square
9.	1 runner	2½" x 24½"	rectangle
10.	1 sleigh	2½" x 14½"	rectangle
11.	3 background, 2 runner and 2 sleigh	2½" x 4½"	rectangle
12.	10 background, 2 candy cane, and 1 runner	2½"	square
13.	1 background and 1 candy cane	1½" x 8"	strip
14.	4 background	1¾"	square
15.	2 background	1½"	square

Directions:

1. Cut the 4⅞" squares in half diagonally as shown. Sew the resulting triangles together to make large half-squares in the combinations below. Make one of each.
sleigh-background
bag-background
runner-background

2. Place a 2½" background square right sides together on the runner corner of the runner-background half-square. Sew diagonally, trim outside the stitching to a ¼" seam and press to the background.

3. Place the runner 2½" square on one end of a 2½" x 4½" background rectangle and sew diagonally as shown.

4. Place a 2½" background square on one end of a sleigh 2½" x 4½" rectangle and sew a diagonal seam as shown.

5. Place a 2½" background square on one end of the 2½" x 24½" runner rectangle. Sew a diagonal seam as shown.

8

6. Sew 2½" background squares on the two corners of a long side of the 6½" x 8½" bag rectangle with diagonal seams as shown.

7. Sew the 1½" candy cane and background strips together lengthwise. From this set of strips cut three 2½" sections.

8. Place a candy cane and a background 2½" square right sides together and sew a diagonal seam as shown. Outside the stitching, trim fabric to a ¼" seam. Press to the striped fabric. This is a 2½" half-square. Then place a 1½" background square on the striped corner of this half square and sew diagonally as shown. Trim and press. Make 2 of these.

9. Sew the 1¾" background squares with diagonal seams on all four corners of the ball 4½" square.

10. Assemble according to the piecing diagram.

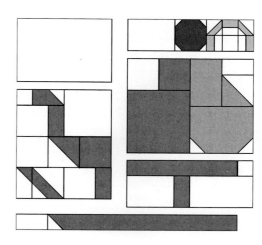

Piecing Diagram

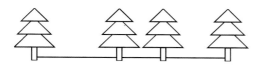

Small Christmas Tree

1½" finished square
15½" x 18½" block with seam allowance

This pattern is given in three different sizes. Be sure the finished square size given at the beginning of the pattern is the same as the finished square size of your quilt.

Cut for 1 block:

1.	4 background	5"	square
2.	2 tree and 2 background	3⅞"	square
3.	2 tree and 2 background	3½" x 5"	rectangle
4.	1 tree and 1 background	3½"	square
5.	2 background	2¾" x 3½"	rectangle
6.	1 tree	2" x 6½"	rectangle
7.	1 tree	2" x 5"	rectangle
8.	2 tree, 1 background, 1 trunk and 1 stand	2" x 3½"	rectangle
9.	11 tree, 9 background, 9 ornament and 2 stand	2"	square
10.	28 tree and 8 background	1"	square

Directions:

1. Cut the background and tree 3⅞" squares in half diagonally as shown. Sew one of each of the resulting triangles together to make a large half-square. Make 3 of these.

2. Place one tree and one background 2" square right sides together and sew a diagonal seam as shown. Trim outside of the stitching to a ¼" seam allowance. This is a 1½" half-square. Make two of these. Make two stand-background half-squares.

3. Place a 2" background square on one end of a 2" x 3½" tree rectangle and sew a diagonal seam as shown. Outside the stitching, trim fabric to a ¼" seam. Press to the dark.

Make one of these sewn to the opposite diagonal.

Make one with reverse fabrics and the opposite diagonal.

4. A. Sew a 2" tree square on one corner of the 5" background square with a diagonal seam. Make 2 of these.

B. Sew a 2" tree square on one corner of the 3½" background square with a diagonal seam. Make another with fabric placement reversed.

C. Sew a 2" tree square to one corner of a 3½" x 5" background rectangle with a diagonal seam according to the diagram. Sew another with the square on the opposite corner. Sew another with the fabric placement reversed.

5. Sew a tree 1" square diagonally on each corner of an ornament 2" square as shown. Trim and press to the dark. Make seven of these. Make two with background 1" squares.

6. Assemble in four horizontal sections according to the piecing diagram.

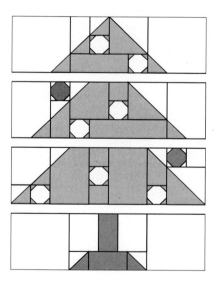

Piecing Diagram

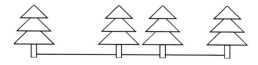 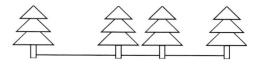

Medium Christmas Tree

2" finished square
20½" x 24½" block with seam allowance

This pattern is given in three different sizes. Be sure the finished square size given at the beginning of the pattern is the same as the finished square size of your quilt.

Cut for 1 block:

1.	4 background	6½"	square
2.	2 tree and 2 background	4⅞"	square
3.	2 tree and 2 background	4½" x 6½"	rectangle
4.	1 tree and 1 background	4½"	square
5.	2 background	3½" x 4½"	rectangle
6.	1 tree	2½" x 8½"	rectangle
7.	1 tree	2½" x 6½"	rectangle
8.	2 tree, 1 background, 1 trunk and 1 stand	2½" x 4½"	rectangle
9.	11 tree, 9 background, 9 ornament and 2 stand	2½"	square
10.	28 tree and 8 background	1⅛"	square

Directions:

1. Cut the background and tree 4⅞" squares in half diagonally as shown. Sew one of each of the resulting triangles together to make a large half-square. Make 3 of these.

2. Place one tree and one background 2½" square right sides together and sew a diagonal seam as shown. Trim outside of the stitching to a ¼" seam allowance. This is a 2" half-square. Make two of these. Make two stand-background half-squares.

3. Place a 2½" background square on one end of a 2½" x 4½" tree rectangle and sew a diagonal seam as shown. Outside the stitching, trim fabric to a ¼" seam. Press to the dark.

Make one of these sewn to the opposite diagonal.

Make one with reverse fabrics and the opposite diagonal.

4. Sew a 2½" tree square on one corner of the 6½" background square with a diagonal seam. Make 2 of these.

5. Sew a 2½" tree square on one corner of the 4½" background square with a diagonal seam. Make another with fabric placement reversed as shown.

6. Sew a 2½" tree square to one corner of a 4½" x 6½" background rectangle with a diagonal seam according to the diagram. Sew another with the square on the opposite corner. Sew another with the fabric placement reversed.

7. Sew a tree 1⅛" square diagonally on each corner of an ornament 2½" square as shown. Trim and press to the dark. Make seven of these. Make two with background 1⅛" squares.

8. Assemble in four horizontal sections according to the piecing diagram.

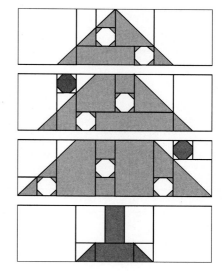

Piecing Diagram

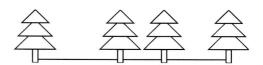

Large Christmas Tree

This pattern is given in three different sizes. Be sure the finished square size given at the beginning of the pattern is the same as the finished square size of your quilt.

Cut for 1 block:

1.	4 background	9½"	square
2.	2 tree and 2 background	6⅞"	square
3.	2 tree and 2 background	6½" x 9½"	rectangle
4.	1 tree and 1 background	6½"	square
5.	2 background	5" x 6½"	rectangle
6.	1 tree	3½" x 12½"	rectangle
7.	1 tree	3½" x 9½"	rectangle
8.	2 tree, 1 background, 1 trunk and 1 stand	3½" x 6½"	rectangle
9.	1 tree, 2 background and 1 stand	3⅞"	square
10.	9 tree, 6 background, 9 ornament	3½"	square
11.	28 tree and 8 background	1½"	square

Directions:

1. Cut the background and tree 6⅞" squares in half diagonally as shown. Sew one of each of the resulting triangles together to make a large half-square. Make 3 of these.

Cut one tree and one background 3⅞" square in half diagonally and sew resulting large triangles together to make two 3½" tree-background half-squares. Make two stand-background half-squares.

2. Place a 3½" background square on one end of a 3½" x 6½" tree rectangle and sew a diagonal seam as shown. Outside the stitching, trim fabric to a ¼" seam. Press to the dark.

Make one of these sewn to the opposite diagonal.

Make one with reverse fabrics and the opposite diagonal.

3. Sew a 3½" tree square on one corner of the 9½" background square with a diagonal seam. Make 2 of these.

4. Sew a 3½" tree square on one corner of the 6½" background square with a diagonal seam. Make another with fabric placement reversed.

5. Sew a 3½" tree square to one corner of a 6½" x 9½" background rectangle with a diagonal seam according to the diagram. Sew another with the square on the opposite corner. Sew another with the fabric placement reversed.

6. Sew a tree 1½" square diagonally on each corner of an ornament 3½" square as shown. Trim and press to the dark. Make seven of these. Make two with background 1½" squares.

7. Assemble in four horizontal sections according to the piecing diagram.

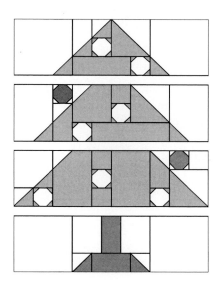

Piecing Diagram

Christmas Beauty

All fabric 42" wide prewashed.
Fabric requirements:
¼ yd. background fabric
⅛ yd. tree fabric (a mix of green fabrics)
2" x 3½" trunk fabric
2" x 10" strip of stand fabric
nine 2" squares of ornament fabric
     (bright colors or lame')
¼ yd. fabric for corner squares
⅓ yd. border fabric

Directions:
1. Make one Small Christmas Tree block according to the directions on pg. 10. (based on 1½" finished square)

2. Cut :

4	5"	corner squares
2	5" x 15½"	top and bottom border
2	5" x 18½"	left and right border

Measure the Christmas Tree block three times across the width. If the average of these measurements is different from the length of the top and bottom border, adjust the border measurement to match. Follow the same procedure for the height measurements. Sew a corner square on each end of the short border sections. Sew on the left and right borders first, then the top and bottom border sections to complete the wall hanging.

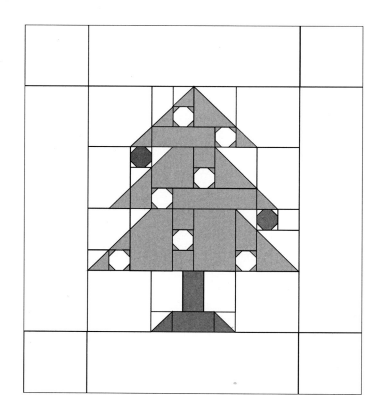

Here Comes Santa Claus; *75 1/2" x 86". Peppermint colors and the traditional hominess of nine-patch blocks in the Irish Chain pattern add a country touch to this design. Give a grownup (even yourself) the pleasure of sleeping under a Santa quilt for the Christmas season. Hand quilted by Tammy Christman.*

St. Nick; 33" x 43". (top left) This jolly elf could be hung on the wall for a month before Christmas to motivate children to extra goodness. Then put up a tree near him and it's almost as if he brought it down the chimney. Pieced and hand quilted by Joan Dawson.

O Tannenbaum; 36½" x 42½". (top right) Silks and metallics, the drama of black and bright colors, and soft-edged bows add an unexpected look to a traditional Christmas subject. What a festive glow from this little tree! This wall hanging will add warmth to the house in the dark month of December. Pieced and machine quilted by Darlene Swenson.

Christmas Beauty; 24½" x 27½". (right) The perfection of this little tree stirs memories of a child's special wishes on Christmas Day. Fabrics woven or printed with gold gleam like ornaments and firelight.

Merry Christmas; *60½" x 74½". The Santa block, Sleigh block, and Christmas Tree block go together to make a complete Christmas statement. Whether you put it on a bed or hang it on a wall, you'll know that Christmas is coming when you get this quilt out every year. Pieced and machine quilted by Joan Dawson.*

Christmas Trees Quilt;
64½" x 72½". A perfect quilt
for bed or nap time. (It may
stay for a month after Christmas because it's hard to let fun
go.) Or glitz up a wall in the
Christmas season to add
excitement to a special time.
Careful choice of fabrics put
different ornaments on each
tree, and Christmas trees all
over this quilt. Pieced by Jean
Look-Krischano. Barbara
Ford lightly stuffed each
ornament with batting before
machine quilting, and glittering metallic thread was used to
add ribbon swags to each tree.

Ho-Ho-Ho; 45½" x 38".
Snowflakes and stars on
almost all the fabrics make
Santa look as if he's
standing in a snowstorm
while he loads his sleigh.
The glittering fabrics in the
quilt and binding add to
the icy look. Hand quilted
by Laura Collier.

St. Nick

All fabric 42" wide prewashed.
Fabric requirements:
¼ yd. red
¼ yd. background fabric
⅛ yd. boot fabric
⅛ yd. white fabric (includes beard)
⅛ yd. inner border fabric
¼ yd. fabric for corner squares
½ yd. border fabric

Directions:
1. Piece one Large Santa block according to the directions on pg. 4. Add a 1½" inner border.

2. Cut: *(You may wish to measure the block with inner border and adjust these outer border pieces to match.)*

A.	2 border fabric	6½" x 20½"
B.	2 border fabric	6½" x 30½"
C.	4 corner squares	6½"

3. Sew the corner squares on both ends of the short border sections. Sew the long border sections on the left and right of the Santa block. Then sew the borders with the corner squares on to top and bottom to complete the quilt top. Enjoy the Christmas Season with Santa.

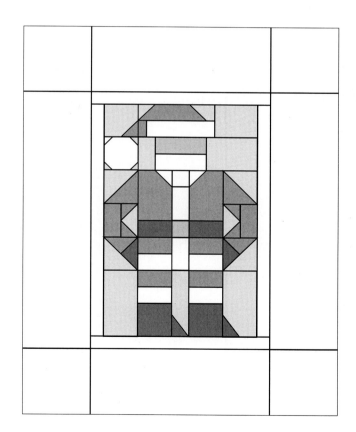

Christmas Trees Quilt

> ## 2" finished square
> Quilt with borders: 64½" x 72½"

All fabric 42" wide prewashed.
Fabric requirements:
1 yd. tree fabric
1 yd. background fabric
2½" strip each trunk and stand fabric
ornament fabric (thirty-six 2½" squares)
¼ yd. fabric for corner squares
1 yd. fabric for setting strips
1¾ yd. border fabric

Directions:
1. Piece four Medium Christmas Tree blocks according to the directions on pg. 12.

2. Cut :

A.	6	4½" x 20½"	setting strips
B.	6	4½" x 24½"	setting strips
C.	9	4½"	corner squares

Measure the blocks and adjust the length of the setting strips if necessary to match the average length and width of the blocks. Sew the trees and long setting strips together alternately into two horizontal rows according to the quilt diagram. Sew the shorter setting strips into three horizontal rows, alternating with the corner squares. Sew all the rows together and add a final 6½" border to complete the quilt.

Christmas Trees Quilt

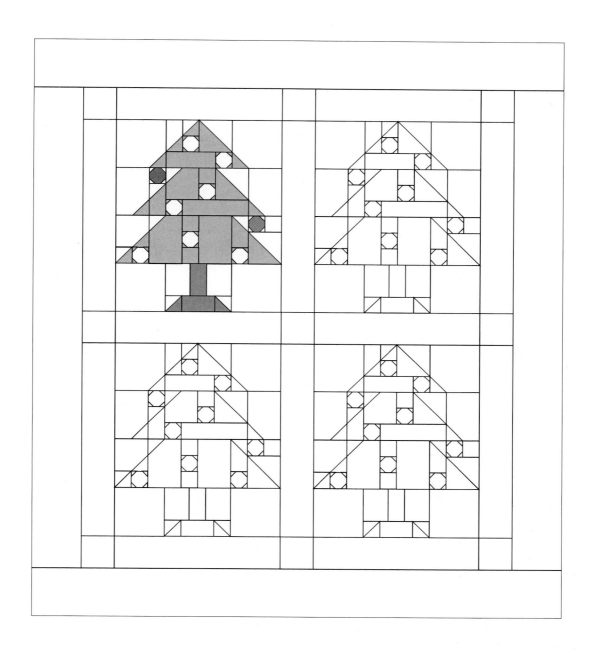

Ho-Ho-Ho

1½" finished square
Quilt with borders: 45½" x 38"

All fabric 42" wide prewashed.
Fabric requirements:
¼ yd. red fabric
¼ yd. Santa background fabric
¼ yd. sleigh fabric
¼ yd. bag fabric
⅛ yd. sleigh runner fabric
⅓ yd. sleigh background fabric
⅛ yd. white fabric
⅛ yd. boot fabric
2" strip each face, beard, candy cane and buckle fabric
⅛ yd. setting strip fabric
⅓ yd. inner border fabric
1 yd. border fabric

Directions:
1. Piece one Small Santa block (pg. 2) and one Small Sleigh block (pg. 6) according to the directions. Both are based on a 1½" finished square.

2. Cut one of each setting strip or border piece according to the directions below. Use scraps or fat quarters to get a nice mix of dark, light, or Christmas fabrics.

A.	setting strip	3½" x 21½"	top of sleigh
B.	setting strip	2" x 21½"	between blocks
C.	inner border	3½" x 36½"	top of blocks
D.	inner border	5" x 36½"	bottom of blocks

Tip: Measure the blocks and tops in three places across the width or height, and adjust the strip to match the average measurement.

3. Add a final 6½" border to complete the wall hanging.
Tip: To make a border with corner squares, cut four 6½" squares. Measure the height of the quilt top in three places and average it. Then cut two 6½" border strips this length. Measure the width of the quilt top in three places and average it. Cut two 6½" border strips this length. Sew the shorter strips onto the left and right sides of the quilt. Sew the corner squares onto both ends of the longer strips and sew them to the top and bottom to complete the wall hanging.

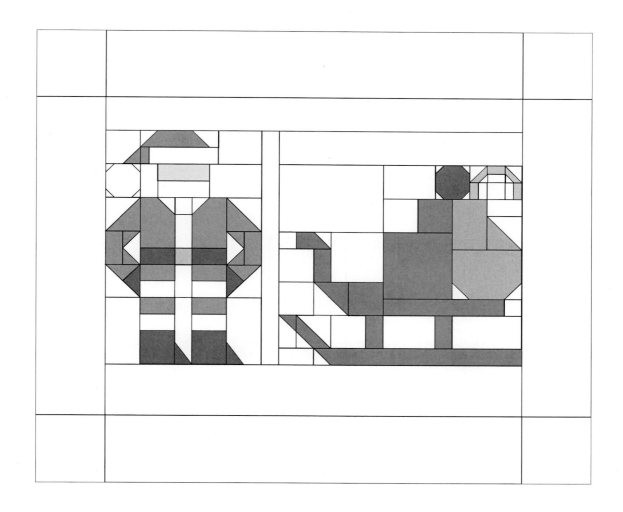

Merry Christmas

All fabric 42" wide prewashed.
Fabric requirements:
½ yd. each tree and tree background fabric
⅓ yd. each red fabric and white fabric
⅓ yd. Santa background fabric and sleigh background fabric
¼ yd. each sleigh fabric, bag fabric, and sleigh runner fabric
¼ yd. each boot fabric and tree trunk fabric
2½" strip each face, beard, candy cane, and tree stand fabric
2½" square buckle fabric
4½" square ball fabric
⅓ yd. each setting strip fabric and inner border fabric
¾ yd. middle border fabric
1¼ yd. outer border fabric

Directions:
1. Piece the blocks below according to the directions on the pages given. All are based on a 2" finished square.
Large Santa pg. 4
Large Sleigh pg. 8
Medium Christmas Tree pg. 12

2. Cut:

A.	8 white	4½"	square
B.	5 red	4½"	square
C.	5 green	4½"	square

From these squares, piece two 9-Patch blocks as shown, one red and one green. Sew the two blocks together in a vertical row and sew this to the left of the sleigh.

3. Cut and sew on each setting strip:

4½" x 20½"	top of tree
2½" x 28½"	between tree and Santa
2½" x 40½"	between top and bottom section

Tip: Measure the blocks and sections in three places across the width or height the strip is matching, and adjust the strip to match the average measurement.

4. Add a 1½" inner border next to the blocks as shown, a 2½" middle border, and a final 6½" border to complete the quilt top.

O Tannenbaum

All fabric 42" wide prewashed.

Fabric requirements:
¾ yd. tree fabric
1 yd. background fabric
⅛ yd. each trunk fabric and stand fabric
ornament fabric (nine 3½" squares of bright colors or lame')
¼ yd. fabric for corner squares
1 yd. border fabric

Directions:
1. Make one Large Christmas Tree Block according to the directions on pg. 14. (Block is based on 3" each finished square.)

2. Cut :

A.	4	3½"	corner squares
B.	2	3½" x 30½"	top and bottom border pieces
C.	2	3½" x 36½"	left and right border pieces

Measure the Christmas Tree block three times across the width. If the average of these measurements is different from the length of the top and bottom border, adjust the border measurement to match. Follow the same procedure for the height measurements. Sew a corner square on each end of the short border sections. Sew on the left and right borders first, then the top and bottom border sections to complete the wall hanging.

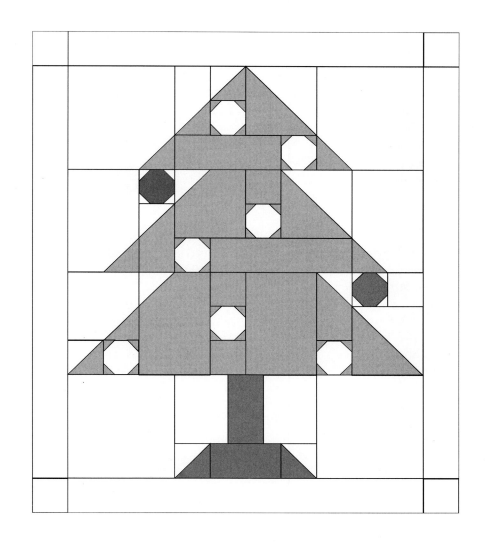

Here Comes Santa Claus

All fabric 42" wide prewashed.
Fabric requirements:
1 yd. Santa background fabric
⅛ yd. beard fabric
2¼ yds. white fabric
⅓ yd. boot fabric
¼ yd. floor fabric
2" strip each face and buckle fabric
1 yd. setting strip fabric
1¾ yds. red fabric
¾ yd. green fabric
1 yd. fabric for alternate squares
1 yd. fabric for setting strips
⅛ yd. fabric for corner squares

Directions:

1. *Note: if all Santa blocks are being made from the same fabrics, first cut a red 2" strip and a white 2" strip. Seam these two strips together lengthwise and then cut 3½" sections from this set of strips for the coat bottom and the boot tops. You will need 24 altogether (two sets of strips).* Piece six Small Santa blocks (pg. 2) based on a 1½" finished square. Cut six 2" x 14" strips of floor fabric and sew one onto the bottom of each Santa block.

2. For the 9-Patch blocks cut:

5	red	2" strips
5	green	2" strips
8	white	2" strips

Sew into sets of strips and then cut into 2" sections according to the chart given below.

1 set	white-red-white	48	2" sections
1 set	white-green-white	48	2" sections
2 sets	red-white-red	96	2" sections
2 sets	green-white-green	96	2" sections

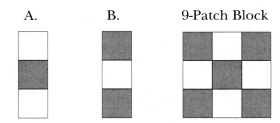

1½" finished square
Quilt with borders: 75½" x 86"

A. B. 9-Patch Block

3. Make a 9-Patch block as shown from one (A.) and two (B.) You will have approximately 42 of these 9-Patch blocks. *You will not get quite all the sections needed. To make the rest cut one green 2" strip and one white 2" strip. Sew together lengthwise. Cut this into 2" sections. (18 needed) Cut 12 green 2" squares and 6 white 2" squares. Add the squares to the cut sections to make the needed parts of the remaining six 9-Patch blocks, and complete the blocks. Or make another complete pair of sets of green strips.*

4. Cut 42 alternate fabric 5" squares. Piece 6 panels in the 9-Patch pattern as shown. Mix and match red or green 9-Patch blocks to get the effect you desire. Each panel has eight blocks and seven alternate squares.

5. Cut:

6	3½"	corner square
8	3½" x 14"	setting strip
9	3½" x 23"	setting strip

6. Sew Santa blocks and panels together with corner squares and setting strips as shown in the quilt diagram. Add a final 6½" border to complete the quilt top. *Tip: Measure the blocks and panels in three places across the width or height the strip is to be sewn on to, and adjust the strip to match the average measurement.*

Cutting and Piecing

General Directions
Tools

You may already have most of the tools needed to piece the quilts in this book. But they will be listed and discussed one by one below so that everything necessary is ready when you begin to make your blocks.

The **rotary cutter** is what makes these patterns quick. Choose the brand and size that is comfortable for you to use and learn how to assemble and clean it. The author prefers a middle-sized Olfa® cutter. After using your rotary cutter carefully for a while, you will no longer dull the blade with little nicks from running over pins, etc.

Rotary Cutter

You will need a **cutting mat** that will keep the rotary blade sharp and protect the table or counter top. Mats come in various colors, with or without rulings on both sides. Choose a color that is easy for you to look at. Rulings are great, but at first you may wish to check the measurements of cut pieces, as the rulings on mats are sometimes not accurate.

Mats come in many sizes, too. One of the larger sizes is good for protecting a table at home, but a smaller size works better for carrying to class. (Don't leave a cutting mat in a car on a warm day.) Eventually a well-used mat will need to be replaced. But first try turning it over and wearing out the back of the mat also.

Be sure to cut at a table or counter that's the right height for you!

There are many **rulers** that work with rotary cutters. Three favorites are the 6" x 12", the 6" square (#6A), and the 9½" square by Omnigrid®.

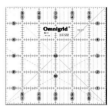

The 6" square is a nice size to work with.

After all the pieces are cut, you will need a sewing machine that takes a nice straight stitch, perhaps a press cloth, and an iron and ironing board.

Easy Cutting and Piecing
Strips, Squares, and Rectangles

Cut a strip first, then cut the strip into all the shapes you need. Begin by pressing pre-washed fabric selvage to selvage. Then bring the fold to the selvages and press again. Use a 6" x 12" ruler to cut a strip the desired width. The short cut needed (12" rather than 24") helps keep the ruler and the rotary cutter under your control.

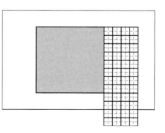

Trim edge straight, then cut the strip.

Use the top ruler edge, bottom ruler edge, or a measuring line across the ruler or on the cutting board to keep the fabric straight. Use the same ruler or perhaps a smaller square ruler to cut off the squares or rectangles needed.

TIP: If you do get a strip that's a little zigzag, you can still cut some pieces from it (but not at the places where the strip is not straight).

Get the Most From Your Fabric

First you will usually cut a strip to match the narrowest measure of the biggest piece. Then look for other needed pieces of the same fabric that share this strip width and cut them next.

Example: The largest piece needed is a 6½" square. So you cut a 6½" strip and cut the squares. Further down the list you see a piece needed from the same fabric that measures 2½" x 6½". So you can cut 2½" wide pieces from the same width.

Then trim the strip to the next width needed, and cut as many pieces from that width as possible. Often you'll be able to get all the pieces needed out of the first strip you cut.

Tip: Also look for pieces where two will fit into the width. Say you had a strip width of 4½", and you needed some pieces 2" x 6½". You could cut a piece 4½" x 6½", trim to 4", and get two of the smaller pieces from it. Generally cut all the largest pieces first, before trimming any width from the strip.

Shape Recognition

You will gradually begin to recognize the various sizes and shapes that you are cutting, and be able to pick them up as needed. But don't hesitate to check measurements with a ruler before sewing one piece on to another.

TIP: To prevent confusion when cutting pieces for a complex pattern, stack all pieces of the same size and pin them together. Write the size on a Post-It® and stick it on top.

Square On Square™ Piecing

As always, use a ¼" seam for piecing.

No small triangles are used when piecing these blocks. Instead, squares are used, and sewn diagonally onto square corners of other squares or rectangles.

For example, the ornament for the Christmas Tree (tree patterns on pgs. 10-15) begins as a large colored square. A small square of background or tree fabric is placed on one corner of the large square, right sides together and lined up accurately. Then a seam is sewn diagonally across the small square, sewing it to the larger piece. The fabrics **outside** the stitching line are trimmed to a ¼" seam and the corner pressed out.

Octagon Inside a Square

Sewing and trimming all four corners results in an octagon inside a square. These pieces are much easier to cut and to handle than little triangles and angled pieces.

The Most Important Seam

Square On Square™ piecing often will require the quilter to sew a diagonal seam across a small square. You can learn to eyeball and just sew the correct seam line, or try one of the following tips:

Tip: Draw a diagonal line on the back of the fabric square with pencil, chalk, or a wash-out marker.

TIP: Fold and crease the square from corner to corner to make a sewing line.

TIP: Use a ruler to draw a line with a permanent fine-tip marker (some colors do wear off after a while) on your sewing machine in front of the needle. The line should be perpendicular to the straight front edge of the sewing machine.

TIP: If you need two large half-squares in the same fabrics, don't cut the light and dark squares in half. Instead, lay the light and dark squares right sides together, draw a diagonal line on the back of the light fabric square with pencil or a wash-out marker, and sew a ¼" seam on each side of this line. Then cut along the pencil line for two pre-sewn large half-squares.

Large Half-Squares (Big Triangles)

A half-square is a square divided in half diagonally (two big triangles sewn together). Usually one half is dark and the other half is light. Big triangles are relatively simple to work with. They are obtained by cutting a square the size given and then cutting the square in half diagonally using a ruler and rotary cutter.

This triangle is then sewn to a triangle of another color, to get a large half-square. This requires sewing two bias edges together. Remember to handle your fabric lightly as you are sewing the triangles together. Many sewing machines sew well straight ahead. Simply laying the two triangles right sides together and gently bringing them under the presser foot with the minimum guidance required allows the machine to do the work.

Practice makes it easier. Even if the seam gets a little stretched in sewing, pressing with a steam iron or wet press cloth generally will correct any distortion.

Small Half-squares

In this book, small half-squares are produced by placing two small squares right sides together and sewing diagonally. The fabrics then are trimmed to a ¼" seam on one side of the stitching. The seam is pressed to the dark. If you need a lot of small half-squares made from the same fabrics, use one of the fast methods for which there are papers or templates.
Ex: Perfect Square™

Half-square It Again

In a few of these patterns, you take the square-on-square technique one step farther. One example: the method used to make Santa's hands. (pg. 4) First a half-square is produced. Then another square of fabric is placed on the half-square, right sides together, and a seam is stiched perpendicular to the seam in the half-square. Care must be taken to trim the excess fabric on the **correct** side of the stitching. This is easier than cutting and seaming three small triangles together. The candy cane (pg. 7) is another example of how to half-square it again.

 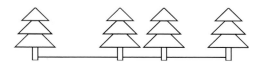

Speedy Strips

Strip piecing is another way to make speed and accuracy easy. To use the candy cane as an example again, three straight sections of the cane are produced by sewing together a 1¼" x 2" striped strip and a 1¼" x 2" background strip. These pieces could be all cut out separately and sewn together, but it is much easier to sew long 1¼" striped strips and background strips together first, press them, and then cut 2" **already sewn** sections from the set of strips.

> TIP: After sewing the long narrow strips together, press the seams to the dark, pulling across the strips as you press to make sure no fabric measurement is lost in the seams. The tip of the iron helps. Then press along the strips, pulling the strip set out straight to correct any distortion from the previous pressing.

Chain Sewing

The author used to have a sewing machine that cut the top thread with each stitch unless there was fabric under the presser foot. So she learned to chain sew. Pieces to be sewn are fed under the needle with minimum space between, and cut apart later. This speeds up the sewing and prevents the messiness of long tails of thread draped everywhere, needing to be trimmed. Many quilters keep a piece of scrap fabric to use at the start (and end) of each chain.

Pressing Techniques

Try a wet press cloth as an alternative to the steam iron. Many experienced quilters feel that using a steam iron distorts the fabric during pressing. Use a dry iron for most of the pressing (perhaps after each seam sewn). This avoids the weight of the iron causing sore elbows and arms during extended piecing sessions.

> TIP: The rule is usually to press to the dark. Occasionally bulky seams make it easier to press to the light.

Then when one block or unit is complete, take a clean piece of old sheet (my favorite, but muslin works too), dampen it in a sink, wring it out, and lay it flat over the pieced block. (The block is right side up.) Run the hot iron lightly but completely over the damp cloth to dampen the block underneath. Then lay the wet press cloth aside, and dry and flatten the block with the hot iron. You may wish to turn the block over afterwards to check that the seams are all laying correctly. Also you can tug at the block a bit as you dry it to square it up. This is like blocking a sweater. Block your block.

Special thanks to these Manufacturers:

Fairfield Processing Corp.
Cotton Batting.......Soft Touch® by Fairfield

Concord House
Fabric

Quilter's Dream Cotton™ Batting
Kelsul, Inc.

Omnigrid, Inc.
Omnigrid® Rulers
Omnimat®

Fasco/Fabric Sales Co., Inc.
Fabric - Marsha McCloskey's Staples®
Fabric - Nancy Martin's Roommates®

Perfect Square © by Monica Novini

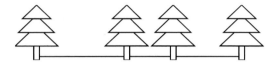 

Also Available From Clearview Triangle:

60° Triangle - Tools For Rotary Cutting
CT1   6" Triangle ruler......................$7.00...............$1.50 s/h
CT2   12" Triangle ruler....................$12.00.............$2.00 s/h
MP3   8" Triangle ruler......................$10.50.............$2.00 s/h
HD4   Half-diamond ruler.................$10.50.............$2.00 s/h

60° Triangle - Books
SF8   Stars & Flowers: Three-sided Patchwork.........$12.95
MA14   Mock Applique'..$15.95
EE7   Easy & Elegant..$15.95
BB10   Building Block Quilts.......................................$14.95
BQ5   Building Block Quilts 2...................................$14.95

Quick Picture Quilts - Books
HH17 Happy Halloween..$9.95

To Order:
Send book cost plus $2.00 s/h first book -
$1 s/h for each additional book to:
    Clearview Triangle
    8311 180th St. S. E.
    Snohomish, WA 98296-4802 USA